Working Words in Spelling

REVISED EDITION

G. Willard Woodruff and George N. Moore
with Robert G. Forest, Donald E. Johnson, Frank DiGiammarino

Great Source Education Group
a Houghton Mifflin Company
Boston, Massachusetts

Become a **S-H-A-R-P** Speller

See
- Look at the word.

Hear
- Say the word.

Adopt
- Close your eyes.
- Spell the word.

Record
- Cover the word.
- Write the word.

Proofread
- Check the word.

Handwriting models in this book are reproduced with permission of Zaner-Bloser, Inc., © 1990.

Printed in the United States of America

International Standard Book Number: 0-669-31387-4

8 9 10 - BA - 99 98 97

A. Beginning Consonants b, m, p

1. Write the two words that begin like **book**.

bell
_____
— — — — — —
_____

fire
_____
— — — — — —
_____

bat
_____
— — — — — —
_____

2. Write the two words that begin like **mouse**.

sun
_____
— — — — — —
_____

man
_____
— — — — — —
_____

mat
_____
— — — — — —
_____

3. Write the two words that begin like **pig**.

pin
_____
— — — — — —
_____

pan
_____
— — — — — —
_____

moon
_____
— — — — — —
_____

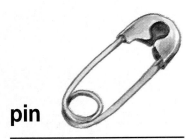

B. Beginning Consonants b, m, p

Say the name of each picture. What sound do you hear at the beginning of the word? Write the word that begins with that sound.

1. **can**
    man
    pan

    _____
    _ _ _ _ _ _ _ _
    _____

2. **bed**
    fed
    red

    _____
    _ _ _ _ _ _ _ _
    _____

3. **ball**
    call
    hall

    _____
    _ _ _ _ _ _ _ _
    _____

4. **fin**
    pin
    win
    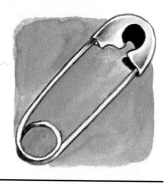
    _____
    _ _ _ _ _ _ _ _
    _____

5. **bat**
    hat
    mat

    _____
    _ _ _ _ _ _ _ _
    _____

6. **fan**
    pan
    tan

    _____
    _ _ _ _ _ _ _ _
    _____

A. Beginning Consonants d, g, s

1. Write the two words that begin like **door**.

milk　　　　　　dog　　　　　　duck

_____　　　　_____　　　　_____

- - - - - -　　　- - - - - -　　　- - - - - -

_____　　　　_____　　　　_____

2. Write the two words that begin like **goat**.

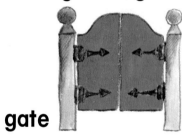

girl　　　　　　gate　　　　　　bee

_____　　　　_____　　　　_____

- - - - - -　　　- - - - - -　　　- - - - - -

_____　　　　_____　　　　_____

3. Write the two words that begin like **six**.

　　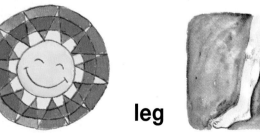

sun　　　　　　leg　　　　　　sand

_____　　　　_____　　　　_____

- - - - - -　　　- - - - - -　　　- - - - - -

_____　　　　_____　　　　_____

B. Beginning Consonants d, g, s

Say the name of each picture. What sound do you hear at the beginning of the word? Write the word that begins with that sound.

1. fun
   run
   sun

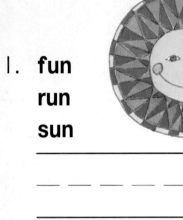

_____

_ _ _ _ _ _

_____

2. came
   game
   name

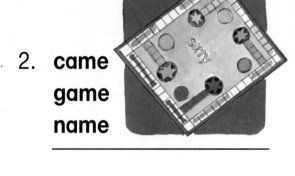

_____

_ _ _ _ _ _

_____

3. dog
   fog
   log

_____

_ _ _ _ _ _

_____

4. dime
   lime
   time

_____

_ _ _ _ _ _

_____

5. hand
   land
   sand

_____

_ _ _ _ _ _

_____

6. boat
   coat
   goat

_____

_ _ _ _ _ _

_____

6

A. Beginning Consonants n, f, l

1. Write the two words that begin like **nose**.

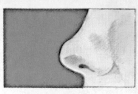

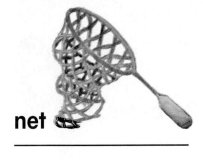

net

rake

nut

_____

__ __ __ __ __ __ __ __

_____

2. Write the two words that begin like **fork**.

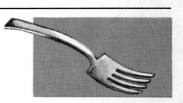

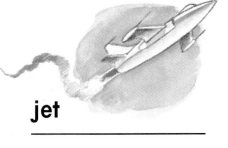

jet

feet

fox

_____

__ __ __ __ __ __ __ __

_____

3. Write the two words that begin like **leaf**.

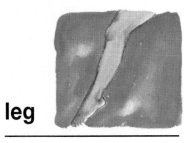

leg

log

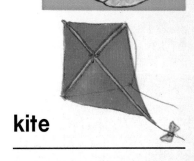

kite

_____

__ __ __ __ __ __ __ __

_____

7

B. Beginning Consonants n, f, l

Say the name of each picture. What sound do you hear at the beginning of the word? Write the word that begins with that sound.

1. dish
   fish
   wish
   _____
   - - - - - - - - -
   _____

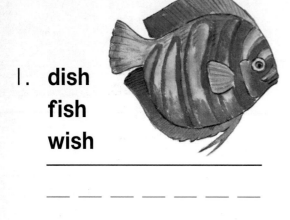

2. but
   cut
   nut
   _____
   - - - - - - - - -
   _____

3. fan
   ran
   tan
   _____
   - - - - - - - - -
   _____

4. cake
   lake
   rake
   _____
   - - - - - - - - -
   _____

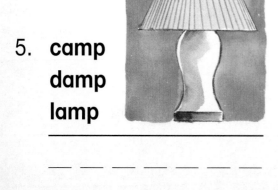

5. camp
   damp
   lamp
   _____
   - - - - - - - - -
   _____

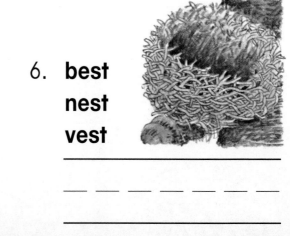

6. best
   nest
   vest
   _____
   - - - - - - - - -
   _____

A. Beginning Consonants t, r, h

1. Write the two words that begin like **tent**.

top

box

two

2. Write the two words that begin like **rose**.

nest

rat

run

3. Write the two words that begin like **horse**.

bird

hand

hop

9

B. Beginning Consonants t, r, h

Say the name of each picture. What sound do you hear at the beginning of the word? Write the word that begins with that sound.

1. king
   ring
   wing

   _____

   _ _ _ _ _ _ _ _

   _____

2. hop
   mop
   top

   _____

   _ _ _ _ _ _ _ _

   _____

3. band
   hand
   land
   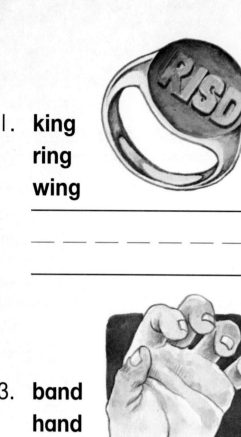
   _____

   _ _ _ _ _ _ _ _

   _____

4. hen
   men
   ten

   _____

   _ _ _ _ _ _ _ _

   _____

5. bat
   hat
   rat

   _____

   _ _ _ _ _ _ _ _

   _____

6. cake
   rake
   take

   _____

   _ _ _ _ _ _ _ _

   _____

A. Beginning Consonants c, w, j

1. Write the two words that begin like **cow**.

cat _____

_____

_____

cup _____

_____

_____

pen _____

_____

_____

2. Write the two words that begin like **worm**.

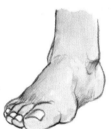 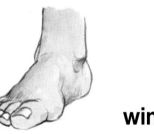

foot _____

_____

_____

wind _____

_____

_____

wood _____

_____

_____

3. Write the two words that begin like **jam**.

jet _____

_____

_____

bell _____

_____

_____

jar _____

_____

_____

B. Beginning Consonants c, w, j

Say the name of each picture. What sound do you hear at the beginning of the word? Write the word that begins with that sound.

1. car
   jar
   tar

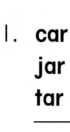

_____

_ _ _ _ _ _ _ _

_____

2. jet
   set
   wet

_____

_ _ _ _ _ _ _ _

_____

3. bell
   sell
   well

_____

_ _ _ _ _ _ _ _

_____

4. bump
   jump
   pump

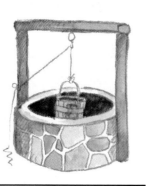

_____

_ _ _ _ _ _ _ _

_____

5. bug
   dug
   jug

_____

_ _ _ _ _ _ _ _

_____

6. can
   man
   pan

_____

_ _ _ _ _ _ _ _

_____

A. Beginning Consonants k, v, y

1. Write the two words that begin like **key**.

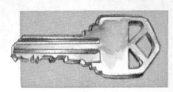

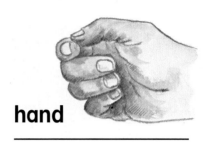 

hand

king

kite

2. Write the two words that begin like **vase**.

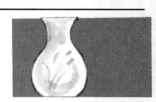

vest

van

bike

3. Write the two words that begin like **yo-yo**.

wind

yarn

yard

B. Beginning Consonants k, v, y

Say the name of each picture. What sound do you hear at the beginning of the word? Write the word that begins with that sound.

1. **king**
   ring
   wing
   _____
   _ _ _ _ _ _ _ _ _
   _____

2. **bite**
   kite
   site

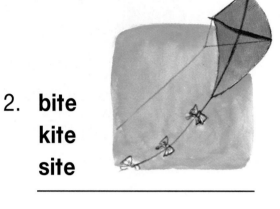

   _____
   _ _ _ _ _ _ _ _ _
   _____

3. **card**
   hard
   yard

   _____
   _ _ _ _ _ _ _ _ _
   _____

4. **ran**
   tan
   van

   _____
   _ _ _ _ _ _ _ _ _
   _____

5. **best**
   rest
   vest
   _____
   _ _ _ _ _ _ _ _ _
   _____

6. **bell**
   fell
   yell

   _____
   _ _ _ _ _ _ _ _ _
   _____

A. Vowel Sounds an, at, all

Write a word that ends with the letters in each hat.
Use each word once.

_____

can

man

bat

hat

ball

fall

_____

_____

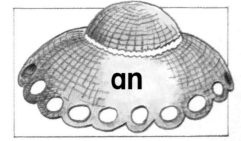

_____

_____

B. Vowel Sounds an, at, all
Find the ending that is missing in each word.
Write the word.

an	at	all

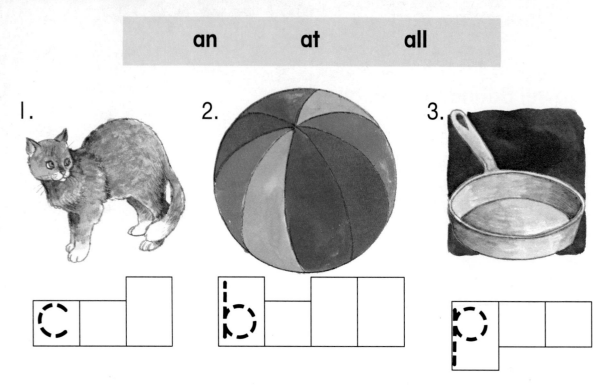

1.

2.

3.

C. Write the two words that have the same ending.

1. call
   tell
   wall

   _____   _____

   - - - - - - - - -   - - - - - - - - -

   _____   _____

2. bag
   fan
   ran

   _____   _____

   - - - - - - - - -   - - - - - - - - -

   _____   _____

3. fat
   pat
   mad

   _____   _____

   - - - - - - - - -   - - - - - - - - -

   _____   _____

16

A. Vowel Sounds et, ed, ell

Write a word that ends with the letters in each bell.
Use each word once.

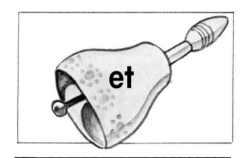

get

pet

bed

red

bell

tell

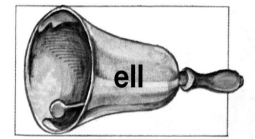

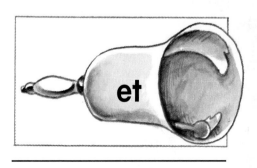

B. Vowel Sounds et, ed, ell

Find the ending that is missing in each word.

Write the word.

et	ed	ell

1.

W [ ] [ ]

2.

j [ ]

3.

b [ ] [ ]

C. Write the two words that have the same ending.

1. **fed**
   sled
   leg

   _____   _____

   _____   _____

2. **tell**
   will
   sell

   _____   _____

   _____   _____

3. **ten**
   let
   wet

   _____   _____

   _____   _____

A. Vowel Sounds it, id, ig

Write a word that ends with the letters in each fish.
Use each word once.

ig

_____

_____

id

_____

_____

bit

sit

it

_____

_____

did

hid

big

ig

_____

_____

dig

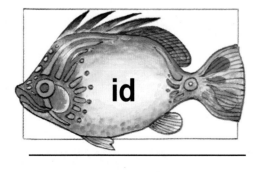

id

_____

_____

it

_____

_____

B. Vowel Sounds it, id, ig

Find the ending that is missing in each word.
Write the word.

it	id	ig

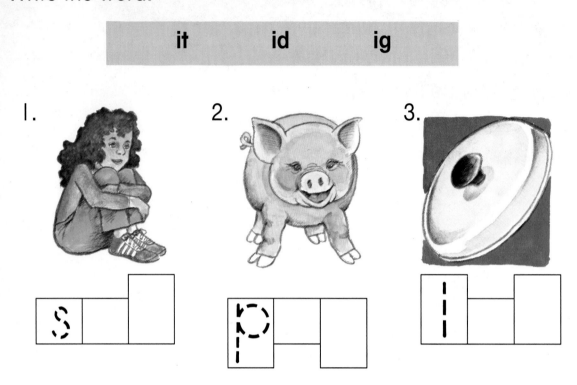

1.

2.

3.

C. Write the two words that have the same ending.

1.
   hid
   dig
   lid

   _____   _____

   _____   _____

2.
   hit
   fit
   pet

   _____   _____

   _____   _____

3.
   did
   wig
   big

   _____   _____

   _____   _____

20

A. Vowel Sounds og, ot, op

Write a word that ends with the letters in each top.
Use each word once.

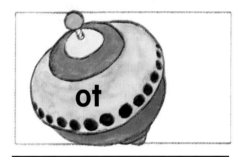

_____

_____

dog

log

got

hot

hop

top

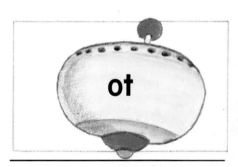

_____

_____

_____

B. Vowel Sounds og, ot, op
Find the ending that is missing in each word.
Write the word.

og	ot	op

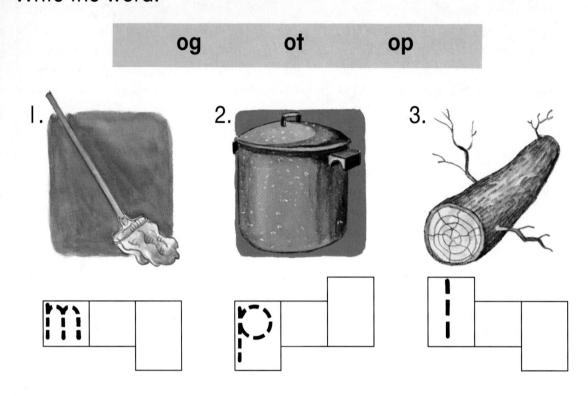

C. Write the two words that have the same ending.

1. pop
   hop
   log
   _____   _____
   _ _ _ _ _ _ _ _ _   _ _ _ _ _ _ _ _ _
   _____   _____

2. fog
   bag
   hog
   _____   _____
   _ _ _ _ _ _ _ _ _   _ _ _ _ _ _ _ _ _
   _____   _____

3. cut
   dot
   hot
   _____   _____
   _ _ _ _ _ _ _ _ _   _ _ _ _ _ _ _ _ _
   _____   _____

A. Vowel Sounds un, ug, ut

Write a word that ends with the letters in each cup.
Use each word once.

fun

run

bug

hug

but

cut

B. Vowel Sounds un, ug, ut

Find the ending that is missing in each word.
Write the word.

un	ug	ut

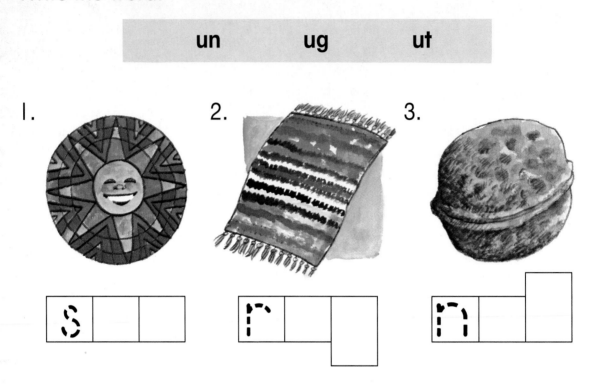

1. s_ _ _

2. r_ _

3. n_ _

C. Write the two words that have the same ending.

1. **cut**
   nut
   bat

   _____ _____

   _____ _____

2. **mug**
   cup
   hug

   _____ _____

   _____ _____

3. **man**
   sun
   fun

   _____ _____

   _____ _____

A. Time to Test. Test your words.

B. Words	**Shapes**	**Write**

1. an

2. man

3. ran

4. at

5. fat

6. cat

C. Words in Sentences

I ate **an** apple.

That **man** is tall.

They **ran** up the hill.

Who is **at** the door?

The pig is **fat**.

We have a tan **cat**.

D. Rhyme Time

Write the spelling words that rhyme.

1. bat, rat, _____ ,

   _____ ,

2. can, pan, _____ ,

   _____ ,

26

Spelling Words

an   man   ran   at   fat   cat

E. Missing Letters

Add the missing letters.
Then write the spelling words.

1. was a kitten   c ___ t   _____

2. like dad   m ___ n   _____

3. big and round   f ___ t   _____

4. went fast   r ___ n   _____

5. I'm ___ home.   ___ t   _____

6. <u>a</u> or ___   ___ n   _____

F. Story Time

Write the spelling words in the story.
Use the number clues to help you.

I	2	3
at	cat	ran
man	fat	an

_____
_ _ _ _ _

There once was a (I) _____ . We saw him

_____
_ _ _ _ _

(I) _____ the park. He had a pet

_____   _____
_ _ _ _ _   _ _ _ _ _

(2) _____ . It was very (2) _____ .

_____
_ _ _ _ _

The man also had (3) _____ old dog. The dog

_____
_ _ _ _ _

(3) _____ after the cat.

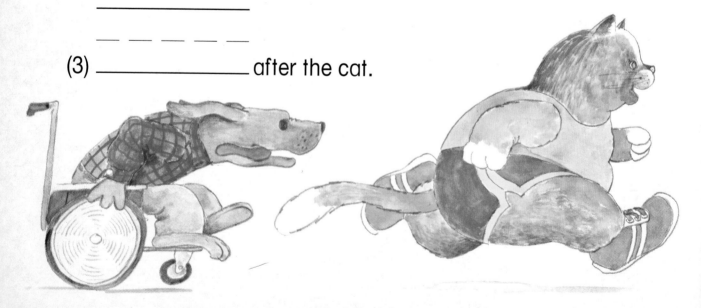

G. I Know My Words. Test your words.

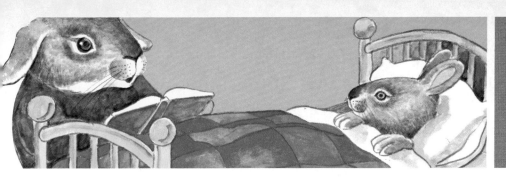

A. Time to Test. Test your words.

B. Words   **Shapes**   **Write**

1. get

2. let

3. pet

4. red

5. bed

6. tell

C. Words in Sentences

I will **get** my book.

Please **let** me go!

We have a **pet** rabbit.

The house is **red**.

My **bed** is small.

Please **tell** us a story!

D. Rhyme Time

Write the spelling words that rhyme.

1. bell, fell, _____

2. led, fed, _____,

3. met, bet, _____,

Spelling Words

get   let   pet   red   bed   tell

E. Missing Letters

Add the missing letters.
Then write the spelling words.

1. a color   r ___ d   _____

2. not <u>give</u>   g ___ t   _____

3. what you
   sleep in   b ___ d   _____

4. an animal
   in your home   p ___ t   _____

5. to say   t ___ ll   _____

6. Please ___
   me in!   l ___ t   _____

F. Sentence Fun

Write the spelling word that fits in each sentence.

1. pet
   tell   I will _____ you something funny.

2. get
   let   They _____ me go with them.

3. red
   pet   My bird is my only _____ .

4. get
   tell   Did you _____ the ball?

5. let
   bed   I am going to _____ .

6. red
   bed   The ball is _____ .

G. I Know My Words. Test your words.

A. Time to Test. Test your words.

B. Words   **Shapes**   **Write**

1. is

2. it

3. bit

4. sit

5. did

6. dig

C. Words in Sentences

Where **is** my hat?   You may **sit** down.

What time is **it**?   Where **did** you go?

I **bit** into the apple.   I will **dig** a hole.

D. Missing Letters

Add the missing letters.

Then write the spelling words.

1. not <u>didn't</u>   d __ d   _____

2. not <u>he</u>
   or <u>she</u>   __ t   _____

3. not <u>stand</u>   s __ t   _____

4. Who ____
   there?   __ s   _____

5. to make
   a hole   d __ g   _____

6. The dog ____
   the bone.   b __ t   _____

Spelling Words

is	it	bit	sit	did	dig

E. Rhyme Time

Write the spelling words that rhyme.

1. hit, fit, _____,

   _____,

2. lid, rid, _____

3. big, pig, _____

4. his, _____

F. Sentence Fun

Write the spelling word that fits in each sentence.

1. bit   _ _ _ _ _
   dig   The dog _____ my hand.

2. it   _ _ _ _ _
   did   Please give _____ to me.

3. dig   _ _ _ _ _
   it   Let's _____ in the sand.

4. is   _ _ _ _ _
   did   I _____ my work today.

5. bit   _ _ _ _ _
   sit   We can _____ here.

6. is   _ _ _ _ _
   sit   My dog _____ big.

G. I Know My Words. Test your words.

A. Time to Test. Test your words.

B. Words   **Shapes**   **Write**

1. on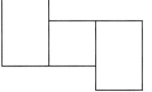

2. dog

3. got

4. pot

5. top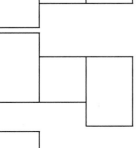

6. hop

C. Words in Sentences

The light is **on**.   Put water in the **pot**.

Our **dog** is black.   Run to the **top** of the hill.

We **got** a new car.   The rabbit can **hop** fast.

D. Rhyme Time

Write the spelling words that rhyme.

1. fog, log, _____

2. mop, stop, _____ ,

3. Don, Ron, _____

4. lot, dot, _____ ,

Spelling Words

on	dog	got	pot	top	hop

E. Missing Letters

Add the missing letters.
Then write the spelling words.

1. a puppy
   that grows up   d __ g   _____

2. a pan with
   tall sides   p __ t   _____

3. to jump on
   one foot   h __ p   _____

4. not <u>gave</u>   g __ t   _____

5. up on ___   t __ p   _____

6. not <u>off</u>   __ n   _____

F. Sentence Fun

Write the spelling word that fits in each sentence.

1. dog
   top   A bird flew to the _____ of the tree.

2. dog
   hop   My _____ is black and white.

3. hop
   top   Let's _____ and skip.

4. on
   pot   Put _____ your coat.

5. on
   got   I _____ a new bike.

6. got
   pot   The _____ is hot!

G. I Know My Words. Test your words.

bed   cat   dog   hop   man   top

A. Name the Picture

Write the spelling word that names each picture.

 = bed    = dog    = man

 = cat    = hop    = top

1.  _____

2.  _____

3.  _____

4.  _____

5.  _____

6.  _____

an   bit   is   let   ran   tell

B. Vowel Code

Change each picture to a letter.
Write the spelling word.

⬤ = a   ◻ = e   △ = i

1. △ s = _____

2. t ◻ ll = _____

3. b △ t = _____

4. l ◻ t = _____

5. ⬤ n = _____

6. r ⬤ n = _____

C. Sentence Writing

Match the parts to make sentences. Write the sentences.
The first one is done for you.

1. We are	coat is **red**.
2. My	is **it**?
3. Where	**at** school.

1. We are at school.

2. _____

3. _____

4. A pig	shoes **on**.
5. Please **sit**	is **fat**.
6. Put your	down.

4. _____

5. _____

6. _____

get   dig   pot   got   did   pet

D. Consonant Boxes

Write the words that begin with each letter.

d	g	p
_____	_____	_____
_____	_____	_____
_____	_____	_____

A. Time to Test. Test your words.

B. Words	**Shapes**	**Write**

1. us

2. fun

3. run

4. sun

5. cup

6. cut

C. Words in Sentences

Are you coming with **us**?
We had **fun** playing games.
Can you **run** fast?

The **sun** is yellow.
Fill the **cup** with water.
I will **cut** the grass.

D. Missing Letters

Add the missing letters.
Then write the spelling words.

1. not <u>work</u>   f __ n   _____

2. not <u>moon</u>   s __ n   _____

3. not <u>them</u>   __ s   _____

4. not <u>walk</u>   r __ n   _____

5. not a <u>glass</u>   c __ p   _____

6. not <u>fix</u>   c __ t   _____

46

Spelling Words

us   fun   run   sun   cup   cut

E. Make a Word

Use the letters to write the spelling words.

—————————   —————————   —————————

—————————   —————————   —————————

F. Sentence Fun

Write the spelling word that fits in each sentence.

1. us
   cut   Will you come with _____?

2. cut
   us   I _____ my paper in two.

3. run
   sun   My dog likes to _____.

4. sun
   run   We sat in the _____.

5. cup
   fun   We are having _____!

6. fun
   cup   I'll fill your _____.

G. I Know My Words. Test your words.

A. Time to Test. Test your words.

B. Words	**Shapes**	**Write**
1. hat		
2. rat		
3. pat		
4. mat		
5. pan		
6. can		

C. Words in Sentences

I have a new red **hat**.   Please step on the **mat**.
We saw a fat **rat**.   Cook the eggs in the **pan**.
I will **pat** the dog.   I **can** jump high.

D. Rhyme Time

Write the spelling words that rhyme.

1. man, ran, _____,
   _____
   _____

2. fat, cat, _____,
   _____,
   _____,
   _____

Spelling Words

hat	rat	pat	mat	pan	can

E. Missing Letters

Add the missing letters.
Then write the spelling words.

1. not a <u>mouse</u> r __ t _____

2. not a <u>pot</u> p __ n _____

3. a rug m __ t _____

4. may c __ n _____

5. not <u>hit</u> p __ t _____

6. a cap h __ t _____

F. Story Time

Write the spelling words in the story.
Use the number clues to help you.

1	2	3
pat	hat	rat
mat	can	pan

_____

— — — — —

We have a pet cat. I like to (1) _____ the cat.

_____   _____

— — — — —   — — — — —

Our pet sits on a (1) _____ . He (2) _____

_____

— — — — —

sit all day. Sometimes he sits in my (2) _____ .

_____

— — — — —

He drinks milk from a (3) _____ . Some days

_____

— — — — —

he goes out to run after a (3) _____ .

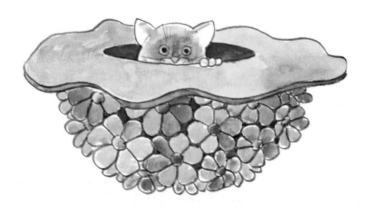

G. I Know My Words. Test your words.

A. Time to Test. Test your words.

B. Words   **Shapes**   **Write**

1. all

2. ball

3. fall

4. hand

5. land

6. sand

C. Words in Sentences

We are **all** here.
Throw the **ball** to me.
How did you **fall** down?

Hold my **hand**.
This **land** is flat.
The **sand** is wet.

D. Rhyme Time

Write the spelling words that rhyme.

1. and, _____,
   _____,
   _____,

2. call, _____,
   _____,
   _____,

Spelling Words

all   ball   fall   hand   land   sand

E. Crossword Puzzle

Write the spelling words in the puzzles.

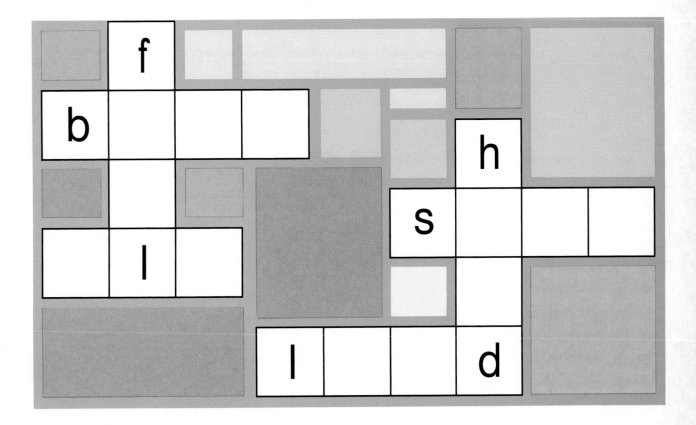

Write the words here.

_____   _____   _____

_____   _____   _____

_____   _____   _____

F. Sentence Fun

Write the spelling word that fits in each sentence.

1. land
   all

   There are many trees on our _____.

2. fall
   hand

   I write with my right _____.

3. all
   ball

   We were _____ playing tag.

4. hand
   sand

   I like to play in the _____.

5. fall
   sand

   Don't let the baby _____!

6. land
   ball

   I threw the _____.

G. I Know My Words. Test your words.

A. Time to Test. Test your words.

B. Words	**Shapes**	**Write**

1. in

2. if

3. him

4. his

5. one

6. said

C. Words in Sentences

The dog is **in** the house.
We will go **if** we can.
What did you say to **him**?

Are those shoes mine or **his**?
I have only **one** pet.
Mother **said** hello to me.

D. Missing Letters

Add the missing letters.
Then write the spelling words.

1. 1   __ n __   _____

2. not <u>out</u>   __ n   _____

3. told   s __ __ d   _____

4. not <u>her</u>   h __ m   _____

5. __ you   __ f   _____
   can

6. not <u>hers</u>   h __ s   _____

58

Spelling Words

in   if   him   his   one   said

E. Crossword Puzzle

Write the spelling words in the puzzles.

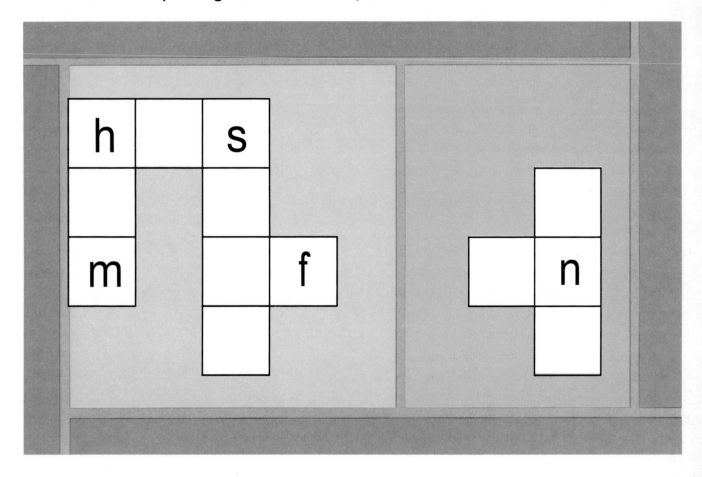

Write the words here.

_____   _____   _____

– – – – – – – – –   – – – – – – – – –   – – – – – – – – –

_____   _____   _____

– – – – – – – – –   – – – – – – – – –   – – – – – – – – –

_____   _____   _____

– – – – – – – – –   – – – – – – – – –   – – – – – – – – –

F. Sentence Fun

Write the spelling word that fits in each sentence.

1. his   ____ ____ ____ ____ ____
   said   I _____ I would play the game.

2. in   ____ ____ ____ ____ ____
   if   We have sand _____ our shoes.

3. if   ____ ____ ____ ____ ____
   one   We can go _____ it's warm.

4. said   ____ ____ ____ ____ ____
   his   He thinks it is _____ ball.

5. in   ____ ____ ____ ____ ____
   him   Do you know _____?

6. him   ____ ____ ____ ____ ____
   one   I have _____ sister.

G. I Know My Words. Test your words.

60

ball   cup   hand   hat   pan   sun

A. Name the Picture

Write the spelling word that names each picture.

= hand

= ball

= sun

= hat

= cup

= pan

1. _____

2. _____

3. _____

4. _____

5. _____

6. _____

all   if   in   land   one   us

B. Vowel Code

Change each picture to a letter.
Write the spelling word.

 = a   = i   = o   = u

1. f = _____

2. s = _____

3. ne = _____

4. n = _____

5. ll = _____

6. l nd = _____

fall   fun   him   his   mat   pat

C. Sentence Writing

Match the parts to make sentences. Write the sentences.

1. Put the **mat**	see **him** at school?
2. Did you	**fun** today.
3. We had	down.

1. _____

2. _____

3. _____

4. I like	**fall** down?
5. Is	to **pat** the dog.
6. Did you	the book **his**?

4. _____

5. _____

6. _____

said   cut   run   can   sand   rat

D. Consonant Boxes

Write the words that begin with each letter.

c	r	s

A. Time to Test. Test your words.

B. Words   **Shapes**   **Write**

1. sat

2. bat

3. had

4. and

5. you

6. the

C. Words in Sentences

Father **sat** down.

Hit the ball with the **bat**.

They **had** to go home.

You **and** I are friends.

May I go with **you**?

Who wrote **the** book?

D. Crossword Puzzle

Write the spelling words in the puzzles.

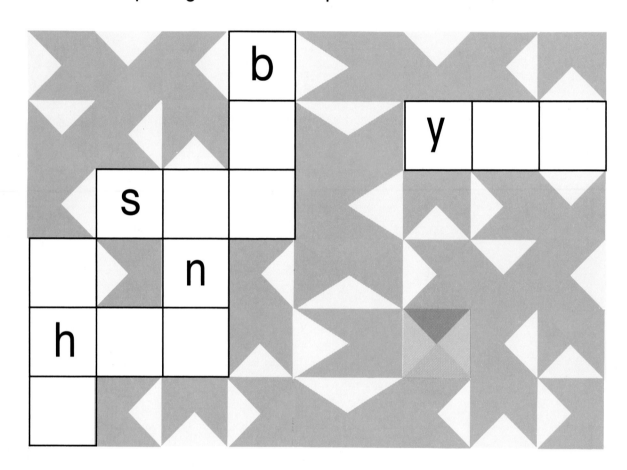

Write the words here.

_____   _____   _____

_ _ _ _ _ _ _ _   _ _ _ _ _ _ _ _   _ _ _ _ _ _ _ _

_____   _____   _____

_ _ _ _ _ _ _ _   _ _ _ _ _ _ _ _   _ _ _ _ _ _ _ _

_____   _____   _____

Spelling Words

sat   bat   had   and   you   the

E. Make a Word
Use the letters to write the spelling words.

_____   _____   _____

‑ ‑ ‑ ‑ ‑ ‑ ‑ ‑ ‑ ‑   ‑ ‑ ‑ ‑ ‑ ‑ ‑ ‑ ‑ ‑   ‑ ‑ ‑ ‑ ‑ ‑ ‑ ‑ ‑ ‑

_____   _____   _____

‑ ‑ ‑ ‑ ‑ ‑ ‑ ‑ ‑ ‑   ‑ ‑ ‑ ‑ ‑ ‑ ‑ ‑ ‑ ‑   ‑ ‑ ‑ ‑ ‑ ‑ ‑ ‑ ‑ ‑

_____   _____   _____

F. Sentence Fun

Write the spelling word that fits in each sentence.

1. and
   you   The boys _____ girls are here.

2. bat
   the   This is _____ day of our play.

3. had
   sat   They _____ a book to read.

4. had
   bat   I have a new _____.

5. you
   and   Where are _____?

6. the
   sat   I _____ down.

G. I Know My Words. Test your words.

A. Time to Test. Test your words.

B. Words   **Shapes**   **Write**

1. up

2. my

3. has

4. was

5. big

6. mom

C. Words in Sentences

We jumped **up** and down.   I **was** late for school.

He is **my** brother.   That is a **big** dog!

Mother **has** two sisters.   My dad and **mom** are home.

D. Make a Word

Use the letters to write the spelling words.

_____   _____   _____

_____   _____   _____

_____   _____   _____

Spelling Words

| up | my | has | was | big | mom |

E. Missing Letters

Add the missing letters.
Then write the spelling words.

1. not <u>little</u>   b __ g   _____

2. not <u>down</u>   __ p   _____

3. not <u>dad</u>   m __ m   _____

4. not <u>is</u>   w __ s   _____

5. not <u>lose</u>   h __ s   _____

6. not <u>your</u>   m __   _____

F. Sentence Fun

Write the spelling word that fits in each sentence.

1. big
   mom   I gave my _____ a hug.

2. up
   has   My friend _____ two dogs.

3. was
   has   Dad _____ happy to see us.

4. up
   my   The kite is _____ in the sky.

5. has
   big   The clown rides a _____ horse.

6. my
   mom   I saw _____ friend at the game.

G. I Know My Words. Test your words.

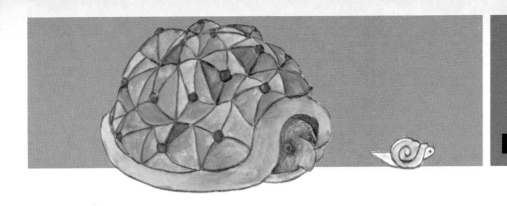

A. Time to Test. Test your words.

B. Words   **Shapes**   **Write**

1. do

2. to

3. am

4. your

5. our

6. out

C. Words in Sentences

How **do** you feel?

We walk **to** school.

I **am** ready to go.

We saw **your** teacher.

This is **our** home.

Is the dog in or **out**?

D. Crossword Puzzle

Write the spelling words in the puzzles.

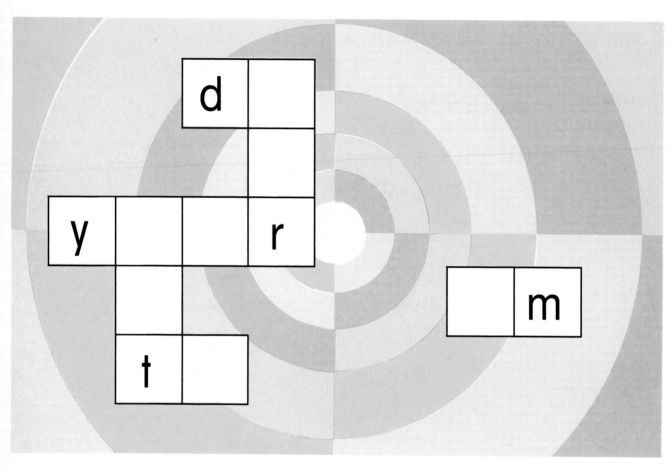

Write the words here.

_____ _____ _____

- - - - - - - - - - - - - - - - - - - - - - - - - - - - - -

_____ _____ _____

_____ _____ _____

- - - - - - - - - - - - - - - - - - - - - - - - - - - - - -

_____ _____ _____

Spelling Words

do   to   am   your   our   out

E. Sentence Fun

Write the spelling word that fits in each sentence.

1. out
   your   Let's look _____ the window.

2. do
   our   What did you _____ today?

3. am
   to   We went _____ the store.

4. our
   out   We do _____ own work.

5. to
   your   Did you cut _____ leg?

6. am
   do   I _____ home.

F. Letter Time

Write the spelling words in the letter.
Use the number clues to help you.

1	2	3
to	out	our
your	do	am

Dear Rosa,

_____

_ _ _ _ _ _

    Please ask (1) _____ mother if you can

_____

_ _ _ _ _

come (1) _____ my house. We can

_____   _____

_ _ _ _ _   _ _ _ _ _

(2) _____ a lot here. We can go (2) _____

_____

_ _ _ _ _

to play. You will like (3) _____ yard. I

_____

_ _ _ _ _

(3) _____ going to be happy if you can come!

                           Your friend,

_____

_ _ _ _ _ _

    Write your name here. _____

G. I Know My Words. Test your words.

76

A. Time to Test. Test your words.

B. Words   **Shapes**   **Write**

1. her

2. for

3. good

4. book

5. look

6. after

C. Words in Sentences

Give the pen to **her**.
This toy is **for** you.
We had a **good** time.

Let's read a **book**.
They **look** at the stars.
We played **after** school.

D. Missing Letters

Add the missing letters.
Then write the spelling words.

1. not <u>him</u>   h __ r   _____

2. not <u>bad</u>   g __ __ d   _____

3. not <u>before</u>   __ ft __ r   _____

4. to <u>see</u>   l __ __ k   _____

5. something
   to read   b __ __ k   _____

6. something
   ___ you   f __ r   _____

Spelling Words

her   for   good   book   look   after

E. Make a Word
Use the letters to write the spelling words.

_____   _____   _____

_____   _____   _____

_____   _____   _____

F. Sentence Fun

Write the spelling word that fits in each sentence.

1. book
    after   I have a new _____ .

2. her
    good   Sara likes _____ dog.

3. for
    look   This gift is _____ you.

4. for
    good   What a _____ day to play!

5. book
    after   We went out _____ dinner.

6. look
    her   Did you _____ at the fish?

G. I Know My Words. Test your words.

bat   book   look   mom   out   up

A. Name the Picture

Write the spelling word that names each picture.

= out

= bat

= look

= up

= mom

= book

 1. _____

 2. _____

3. _____

 4. _____

 5. _____

 6. _____

B. Vowel Code

Change each picture to a letter.
Write the spelling word.

26

 = a   = e   = o

1. t =   _____

2.  m =   _____

3. s  t =   _____

4. f  r =   _____

5. th =   _____

6. g  d =   _____

82

after   and   do   my   our   was

C. Sentence Writing

Match the parts to make sentences. Write the sentences.

1.	These are	are here.
2.	We played	**my** shoes.
3.	Mom **and** Dad	**after** school.

1. _____

2. _____

3. _____

4.	I **was**	did you **do**?
5.	This is **our**	having fun.
6.	What	cat.

4. _____

5. _____

6. _____

had   you   big   her   your   has

D. Consonant Boxes

Write the words that begin with each letter.

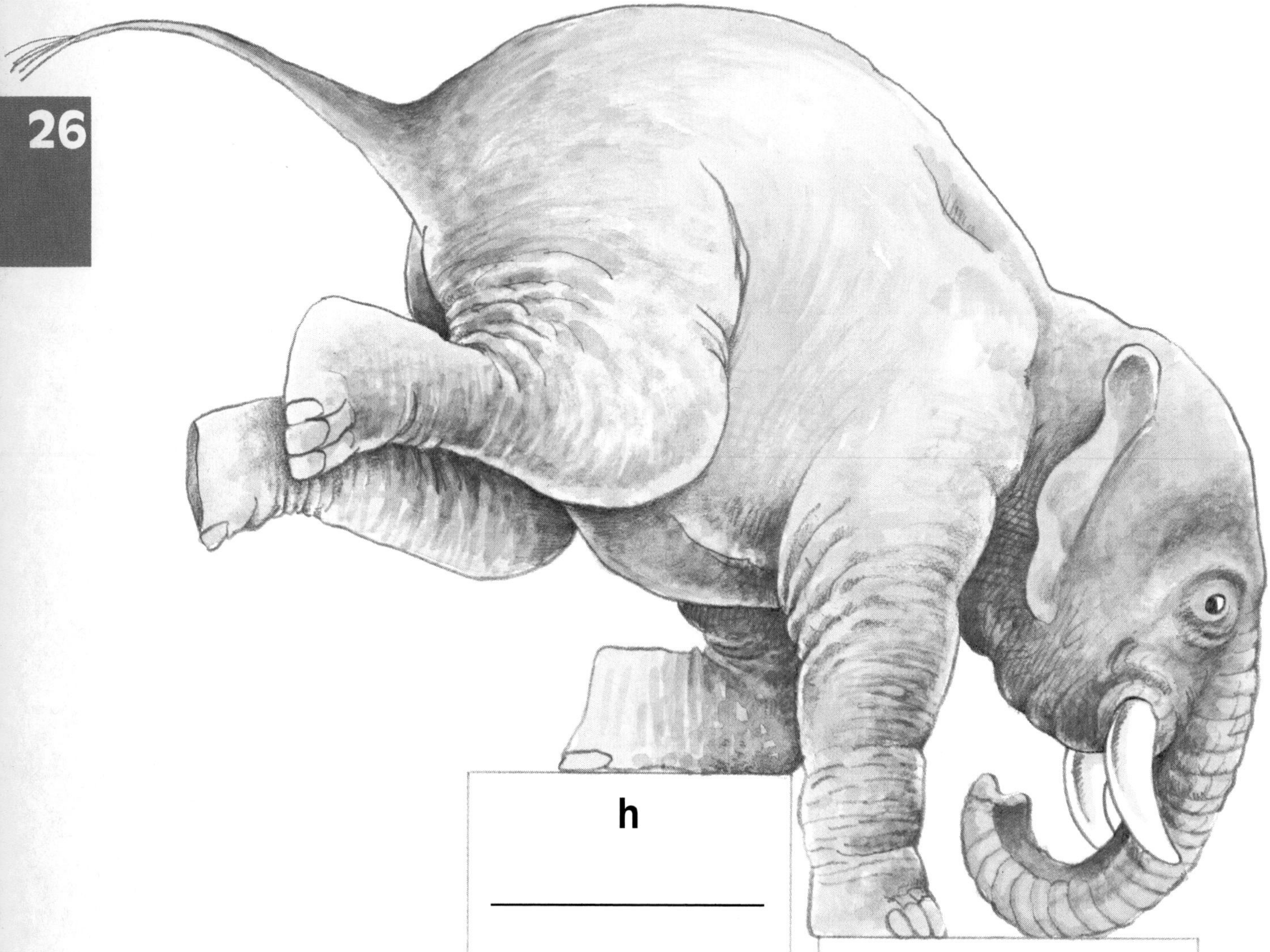

h

_____

- - - - - - - - - - -

_____

_____

- - - - - - - - - - -

_____

_____

y

_____

_____

- - - - - - - - - - -

_____

b

_____

- - - - - - - - - - -

_____

A. Time to Test. Test your words.

B. Words **Shapes** **Write**

1. I

2. ice

3. he

4. she

5. they

6. that

C. Words in Sentences

He and **I** are brothers.
Put **ice** in the glass.
What does **he** want?

Mother said **she** is going.
Who are **they**?
Stop **that** bus!

D. Crossword Puzzle

Write the spelling words that fit in the puzzle.

Write the
words here.

_____

_____

_____

_____

_____

_____

_____

_____

_____

What word was not used?
It is a capital letter.

_____

_ _ _ _ _ _

_____

86

Spelling Words

I   ice   he   she   they   that

E. Missing Letters

Add the missing letters.
Then write the spelling words.

1. me
__ __ __ _____

2. he and she   th __ y
__ __ _____

3. not he   sh __
__ __ _____

4. snow
   and ___   __ c __
__ __ __ __ _____

5. not this   th __ t
__ __ _____

6. not she   h __
__ __ _____

F. Sentence Fun

Write the spelling word that fits in each sentence.

1. she
   that   Does _____ know many songs?

2. ice
   they   Do you know who _____ are?

3. I
   that   May _____ have some milk?

4. ice
   he   I know who _____ is.

5. ice
   they   The _____ is cold.

6. that
   she   I like _____ color.

G. I Know My Words. Test your words.

88

A. Time to Test. Test your words.

B. Words **Shapes** **Write**

1. boy

2. toy

3. me

4. dad

5. girl

6. love

C. Words in Sentences

Their baby is a **boy**.
I have a new **toy**.
Please tell **me** a story.

My **dad** is sleeping.
She is a happy **girl**.
We **love** to sing.

D. Missing Letters

Add the missing letters.
Then write the spelling words.

1. not h<u>ate</u>   l __ v __   _____

2. not a <u>boy</u>   g __ rl   _____

3. not <u>mom</u>   d __ d   _____

4. not a <u>girl</u>   b __ y   _____

5. not <u>you</u>   m __   _____

6. not a <u>book</u>   t __ y   _____

Spelling Words

boy   toy   me   dad   girl   love

E. Make a Word

Use the letters to write the spelling words.

_____   _____   _____

_____   _____   _____

_____   _____   _____

F. Name the Picture
Write the spelling words that name the pictures.

= dad

= toy

= love

= boy

= me

= girl

My _____ and I went to the park. I

brought my new _____ with

_____. We met a _____

and a _____ there. We all played

together. I _____ to go to the park.

G. I Know My Words. Test your words.

A. Time to Test. Test your words.

B. Words   **Shapes**   **Write**

1. we

2. go

3. not

4. off

5. play

6. nice

C. Words in Sentences

When will **we** leave?

Do not **go** away.

They are **not** home.

A light turns on and **off**.

Let's **play** a game.

Our teacher is **nice**.

D. Missing Letters

Add the missing letters.
Then write the spelling words.

1. not on   ___ ff   _____

2. to have fun   pl ___ ___   _____

3. you and I   w ___   _____

4. kind   n ___ c ___   _____

5. sick or
   ___ well   n ___ t   _____

6. to move   g ___   _____

94

Spelling Words

we	go	not	off	play	nice

E. Rhyme Time

Write the spelling words that rhyme.

1. pot, got, _____

2. ice, mice, _____

3. no, so, _____

4. say, way, _____

5. she, he, _____

What word was not used? _____

95

F. Story Time

Write the spelling words that fit in the story.
Use the number clues to help you.

1	2	3
play	we	off
nice	go	not

_____

— — — — — —

I have a (1) _____ dog. She likes to

_____   _____

— — — — —   — — — — — —

(1) _____ ball. Sometimes (2) _____

_____

— — — — — —

go to the park. My dog likes to (2) _____

_____

— — — — — —

down the slide. She does (3) _____ fall

_____

— — — — — —

(3) _____ . She does look funny! What tricks

can your pet do?

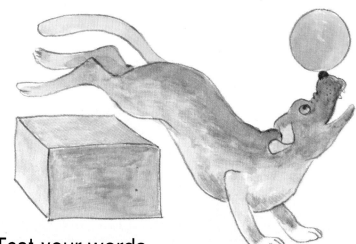

G. I Know My Words. Test your words.

96

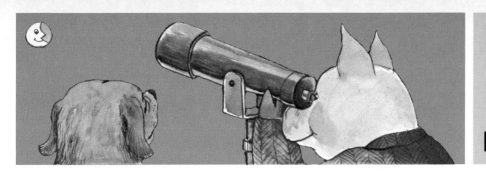

A. Time to Test. Test your words.

B. Words	**Shapes**	**Write**
1. no		
2. so		
3. put		
4. see		
5. eat		
6. yes		

C. Words in Sentences

I shook my head **no**.

I am **so** happy.

Please **put** your toys away.

Did you **see** many stars?

Please **eat** your lunch.

Did you say **yes** or no?

D. Missing Letters

Add the missing letters.

Then write the spelling words.

1. not <u>yes</u>   n ___   _____

2. not <u>drink</u>   ___ ___ t   _____

3. not <u>no</u>   y ___ s   _____

4. to look   s ___ ___   _____

5. to place   p ___ t   _____

6. I like you
___ much.   s ___   _____

Spelling Words

no   so   put   see   eat   yes

E. Crossword Puzzle

Write the spelling words in the puzzles.

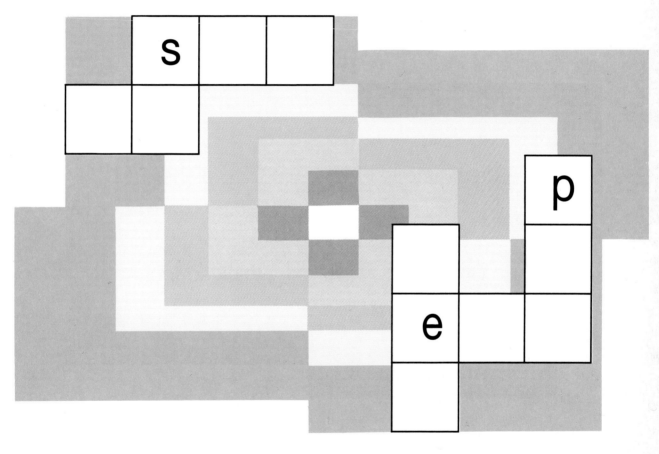

Write the words here.

_____   _____   _____

_____   _____   _____

_____   _____   _____

_____   _____   _____

F. Sentence Fun

Write the spelling word that fits in each sentence.

1. put
   so

   _____

   __ __ __ __ __

   Please _____ your name on your papers.

2. no
   see

   _____

   __ __ __ __ __

   Did you _____ a lion at the zoo?

3. eat
   no

   _____

   __ __ __ __ __

   Is he saying yes or _____ ?

4. eat
   yes

   _____

   __ __ __ __ __

   Is it time to _____ dinner?

5. put
   yes

   _____

   __ __ __ __ __

   Oh, _____ , I think so too!

6. see
   so

   _____

   __ __ __ __ __

   Are you here _____ soon?

G. I Know My Words. Test your words.

boy   dad   eat   ice   play   toy

A. Name the Picture

Write the spelling word that names each picture.

= dad

= play

= boy

= toy

= eat

= ice

31

1.  _____

2.  _____

3.  _____

4. 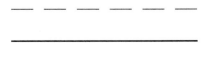 _____

5. _____

6.  _____

101

he   off   put   that   we   yes

B. Vowel Code

Change each picture to a letter.
Write the spelling word.

 = a   = e   = o   = u

31

1. w  = _____

2. p  t = _____

3. th  t = _____

4. y  s = _____

5. ff = _____

6. h  = _____

I   love   me   nice   she   they

C. Sentence Writing

Match the parts to make sentences. Write the sentences.

1. Are **they**	is **nice**.
2. Do you	your friends?
3. My teacher	know **me**?

1. _____

2. _____

3. _____

4. Is	to dance.
5. We **love**	**she** your age?
6. You and **I**	are friends.

4. _____

5. _____

6. _____

31

not   girl   see   no   go   so

D. Consonant Boxes

Write the words that begin with each letter.

g	n	s
_____	_____	_____
_____	_____	_____
_____	_____	_____
_____	_____	_____
_____	_____	_____

A. Time to Test. Test your words.

B. Words   **Shapes**   **Write**

1. went

2. with

3. will

4. now

5. snow

6. saw

C. Words in Sentences

They **went** on a trip.

May I go **with** you?

I **will** help you.

We must leave **now**.

Let's play in the **snow**.

Father **saw** a bear!

D. Missing Letters

Use the letters to write the spelling words.

Spelling Words

went   with   will   now   snow   saw

E. Sentence Fun

Write the spelling word that fits in each sentence.

1. went
   will
   Did you see where they _____?

2. now
   will
   We _____ go with you too.

3. saw
   went
   They _____ many stars.

4. snow
   with
   It will _____ all day.

5. with
   saw
   Take me _____ you.

6. snow
   now
   May I go _____?

F. Story Time

Write the spelling words in the story.
Use the number clues to help you.

1	2	3
snow	with	now
went	saw	will

_____

— — — — — —

Today I (1) _____ out to play. I like to

_____

— — — — —

play in the (1) _____ . My dog Winnie came

_____

— — — — —

(2) _____ me. While we were playing we

_____

— — — — —

(2) _____ a rabbit. Winnie ran after it but the

_____

— — — — —

rabbit was too quick! Tomorrow we (3) _____

_____

— — — — —

look for the rabbit again. For (3) _____ ,

Winnie and I are going to sleep!

G. I Know My Words. Test your words.

A. Time to Test. Test your words.

B. Words	**Shapes**	**Write**

1. day

2. away

3. made

4. make

5. but

6. jump

C. Words in Sentences

This is the **day** of the fair. Did you **make** your bed?

My friend moved **away**. I like snow, **but** not rain.

We **made** kites in school. Let's skip and **jump**!

D. Rhyme Time

Write the spelling word that rhymes with the underlined word in the sentence.

_____

_ _ _ _ _ _ _

1. We wish we could <u>play</u> all night and _____.

_____

_ _ _ _ _ _ _

2. He looked _____ did not find the <u>nut</u>.

_____

_ _ _ _ _ _ _

3. I got a <u>bump</u> when I tried to _____.

_____

_ _ _ _ _ _ _

4. If you <u>bake</u>, what will you _____?

_____

_ _ _ _ _ _ _

5. We <u>stayed</u> to see what you _____.

_____

_ _ _ _ _ _ _

6. Will you <u>stay</u> or go _____?

day away made make but jump

E. Crossword Puzzle

Write the spelling words in the puzzles.

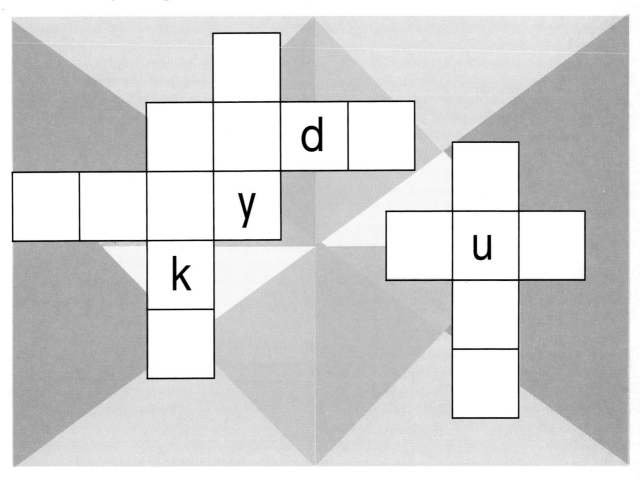

Write the words here.

_____   _____   _____

- - - - - - - - - -   - - - - - - - - - -   - - - - - - - - - -

_____   _____   _____

_____   _____   _____

- - - - - - - - - -   - - - - - - - - - -   - - - - - - - - - -

day away made make but jump

F. Make a Word

Use the letters to write the spelling words.

_____ _____ _____

------------------------ ------------------------ ------------------------

_____ _____ _____

------------------------ ------------------------ ------------------------

_____ _____ _____

G. I Know My Words. Test your words.

A. Time to Test. Test your words.

B. Words **Shapes** **Write**

1. when

2. then

3. them

4. there

5. this

6. thing

C. Words in Sentences

Tell me **when** you are ready.   My dog is over **there**.
I did not know you **then**.   Whose pet is **this**?
I know **them** well.   What is that **thing**?

D. Crossword Puzzle

Write the spelling words in the puzzle.

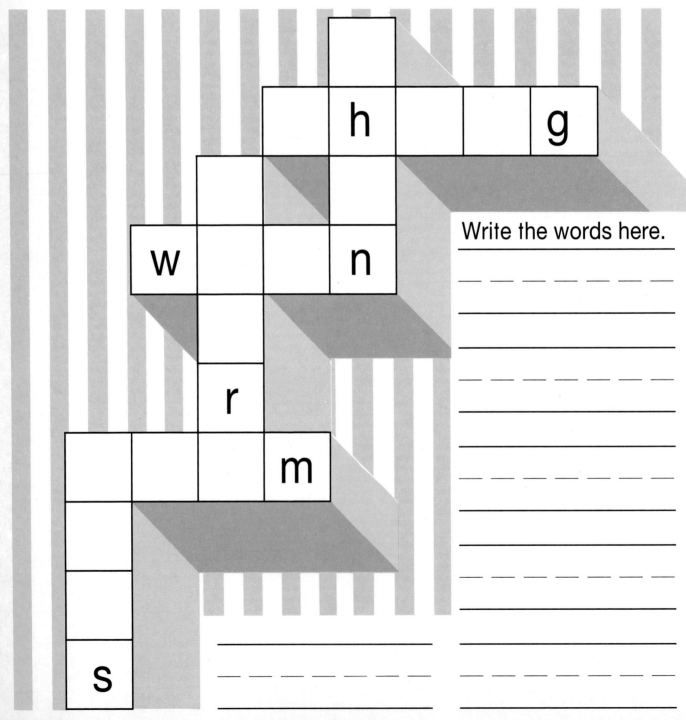

Write the words here.

_____

_____

_____

_____

_____

_____

_____

_____

when then them there this thing

E. Missing Letters
Add the missing letters.
Then write the spelling words.

1. not <u>now</u>   th __ n   _____

2. not an <u>animal</u>   th __ ng   _____

3. not <u>us</u>   th __ m   _____

4. not <u>that</u>   th __ s   _____

5. not <u>here</u>   th __ r __   _____

6. not <u>where</u>   wh __ n   _____

115

F. Story Time

Write the spelling words in the story.
Use the number clues to help you.

I	2	3
there	then	this
when	them	thing

We went to the zoo. We saw the bears

_____   _____

_ _ _ _ _ _ _   _ _ _ _ _

(I) _____ we got (I) _____ .

_____

_ _ _ _ _

We (2) _____ fed some birds. We gave

_____

_ _ _ _ _

(2) _____ bread. What a fun

_____

_ _ _ _ _

(3) _____ to do. I think you would have

_____

_ _ _ _ _

liked (3) _____ trip.

G. I Know My Words. Test your words.

A. Time to Test. Test your words.

B. Words   **Shapes**   **Write**

1. going

2. cow

3. little

4. school

5. mother

6. happy

C. Words in Sentences

We are **going** to the zoo.
Look at the brown **cow**.
My **little** sister is two.

We ride a bus to **school**.
Our **mother** works at a store.
What a **happy** face!

D. Missing Letters

Add the missing letters.
Then write the spelling words.

1. not big   l __ ttl __   _____

2. not <u>father</u>   m __ th __ r   _____

3. not <u>coming</u>   g __ __ ng   _____

4. glad   h __ pp __   _____

5. a place to learn   sch __ __ l   _____

6. a farm animal   c __ w   _____

Spelling Words

going	cow	little	school
mother	happy		

E. Sentence Fun

Write the spelling word that fits in each sentence.

1. happy
   mother

   If I'm her child, she's a _____.

2. happy
   cow

   If it says "Moo," it is a _____.

3. school
   little

   If I'm in class, I'm in _____.

4. cow
   going

   If you leave, you are _____.

5. going
   little

   If it is small, it is _____.

6. happy
   school

   If I smile, I am _____.

F. Name the Picture

Write the spelling words that name the pictures.

= mother

= happy

= school

= going

= cow

= little

We saw a _____

_ _ _ _ _ _ _

_____

_____

_ _ _ _ _ _ _

_____ on our way to

_____

_ _ _ _ _ _ _

_____ today. It did not look

_____

_ _ _ _ _ _ _

_____ . It had lost its

_____

_ _ _ _ _ _ _

_____ . We are

_____

_ _ _ _ _ _ _

_____ to help find its mother.

G. I Know My Words. Test your words.

120

cow   happy   jump   mother   school   snow

A. Name the Picture

Write the spelling word that names each picture.

1. _____

2. _____

3. _____

4. _____

5. _____

6. _____

36

but   day   then   thing   this   when

B. Vowel Code

Change each picture to a letter.
Write the spelling word.

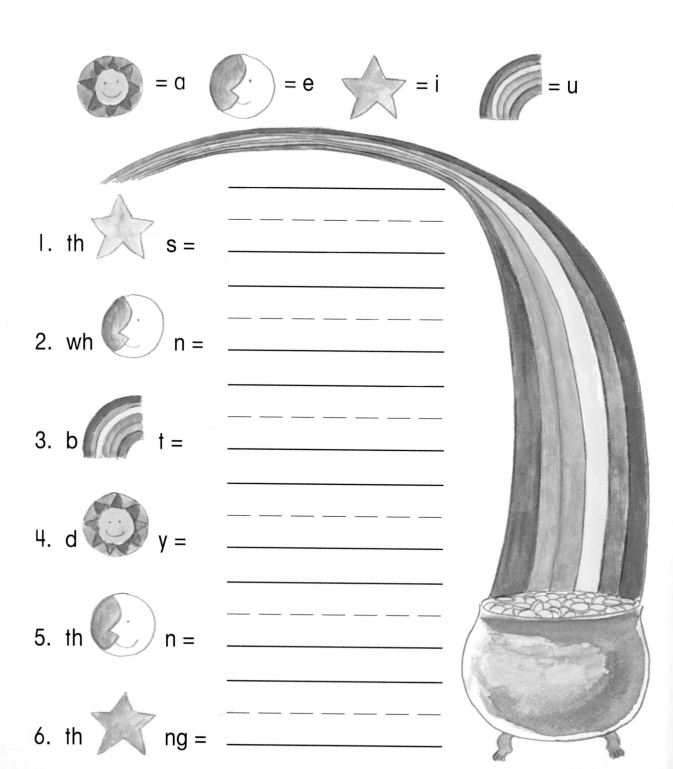

= a   = e   = i   = u

36

1. th ⭐ s = _____

2. wh 🌙 n = _____

3. b 🌈 t = _____

4. d ☀ y = _____

5. th 🌙 n = _____

6. th ⭐ ng = _____

away   going   now   saw   them   there

C. Sentence Writing

Match the parts to make sentences. Write the sentences.

1.	I **saw**	know **them**?
2.	Put the	a bird.
3.	Do you	book **there**.

1. _____

2. _____

3. _____

36

4.	They	the toys **away**.
5.	Put	to school?
6.	Are you **going**	are here **now**.

4. _____

5. _____

6. _____

made   with   little   went   make   will

D. Consonant Boxes

Write the words that begin with each letter.

w
_____
- - - - - - - - - - -
_____
- - - - - - - - - - -
_____

m
_____
- - - - - - - - - - -
_____

l
_____
- - - - - - - - - - -

Spelling Dictionary/WORDFINDER
Level A

The **Spelling Dictionary/WORDFINDER** has all of the words from your spelling book. It tells you how to spell words. It tells you what words mean. Sentences and pictures help you to understand the words.

It is easy to find words in the **Spelling Dictionary/WORDFINDER**. Letters of the alphabet are at the top of each page. The words are in the same order as the letters of the alphabet.

A B C D E F G H I J K L M N O P Q R S T U V W X Y Z

To find a word like **bed**, look for the page with the letters **A-B** at the top. Find the word **bed** in dark print on the page. Then read the sentences under the word. They tell you what **bed** means. Now look at the picture. It shows you what a **bed** is.

at   **A-B**   bed

at
Carlos went to Maria's house.
He is **at** Maria's house now.

away
It takes us a long time to get to the park.
The park is far **away**.

ball
A **ball** is a round toy.
We use a **ball** in many games.

bat
A **bat** is a long, thick piece of wood.
I used the **bat** to hit the ball.

bed
A **bed** is a soft place to sleep.
I sleep in my **bed** at night.

127

after

I had lunch before I went out to play.

I went out to play **after** I ate lunch.

all

We saw a lion, tiger, and bear at the zoo.

We saw **all** of them at the zoo.

am

You are five years old. I **am** six years old.

an

An means the same thing as a. **An** is used in front of words that begin with a, e, i, o, and u. The story is about **an** ant and a bee.

and

And is used to put words together.

Meg has a dog **and** a cat.

at

Carlos went to Maria's house.

He is **at** Maria's house now.

away

It takes us a long time to get to the park.

The park is far **away**.

ball

A **ball** is a round toy.

We use a **ball** in many games.

bat

A **bat** is a long, thick piece of wood.

I used the **bat** to hit the ball.

bed

A **bed** is a soft place to sleep.

I sleep in my **bed** at night.

big

Big means large. A bear is a **big** animal.

bit

Did the baby bite you?

Yes, the baby **bit** me.

book

A **book** is something to read.

It has pages with words or pictures.

boy

A **boy** is a child.

A **boy** grows up to be a man.

but

I am tall. Amy is taller.

I am tall, **but** not as tall as Amy.

can

I know how to tie my shoes.

I **can** tie my shoes.

cat

A **cat** is a small animal with soft fur.

We have a pet **cat**.

cow

A **cow** is a large farm animal.

We get milk from a **cow**.

cup

A **cup** is a short glass. I drink from a **cup**.

cut

Nina pushed a knife through the apple.

She **cut** the apple in two.

129

dad

Dad is another name for father.

I love my mom and **dad**.

day

Day is the time when the sun shines.

When **day** ends, night begins.

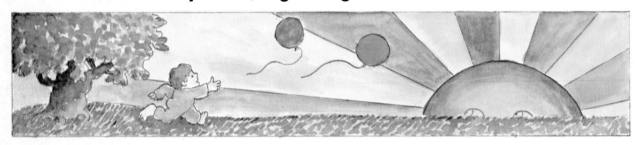

did

I do my work today.

I **did** my work yesterday too.

dig

Dig means to make a hole in the ground.

Dogs **dig** holes for their bones.

do

I need to cut the grass.

I will **do** it tomorrow.

dog

A **dog** is an animal that likes to bark.

A **dog** makes a good pet.

eat

Eat means to put food inside your body.

I **eat** with my mouth.

fall

Fall means to drop.

The apples **fall** from the tree.

fat

Fat means big and round.

A pig is a **fat** animal.

for

I gave you flowers.

The flowers were **for** you.

fun

Fun means having a good time.

We had **fun** at your birthday party.

get

Father will take his hat from its box.

He will **get** his hat from its box.

girl

A **girl** is a child.

A **girl** grows up to be a woman.

go

Go means to move from one place to another.

We **go** from home to school.

going

Alex and Sarah go to the park on nice days.

Today is a nice day.

They are **going** to the park today.

good

We like to play this game.

It is a **good** game to play.

got

What did you get for your last birthday?

I **got** a book.

had

I used to have long hair.

I **had** long hair until I cut it.

hand

A **hand** is a part of the body.

I hold a book in my **hand**.

happy

Happy means glad.

I feel **happy** when I dance.

has

I have brown eyes.

My sister **has** brown eyes too.

hat

A **hat** is something you wear on your head.

I wear a **hat** in the winter.

he

Ben is my friend. **He** is very nice.

her

Do you know Beth? Have you met **her**?

him

Danny needs help. I will help **him**.

his

This is Pedro's hat. It is **his** hat.

hop

Hop means to make a short jump.

Rabbits **hop** on the ground.

I

The red bike is mine.

I have a red bike.

ice

Water turns to **ice** when it gets very cold.

We skate on the **ice**.

if

It may rain. It may not rain.

I will get wet **if** it rains.

in

In means inside. We will stay
in the house until the rain stops.

is

It was raining yesterday.
It **is** sunny today.

it

Where is my book bag?
Did I leave **it** in school?

jump

Frogs use their legs to go high into the air.
Frogs **jump** around the lake.

land

Land is ground.
Grass grows on the **land** around our house.

let

You may play with my toys.

I will **let** you play with them.

little

Little means small.

A mouse is a **little** animal.

look

Look means to use your eyes to see.

I **look** at the clock to see what time it is.

love

1) I like very much to go to the park.

I **love** to go to the park.

2) I care about my family a lot.

I **love** my family.

made

I make animals out of clay.

I **made** a turtle yesterday.

make

Make means to put together.

I **make** mud pies from dirt and water.

man

A **man** is a boy who grows up.

That **man** is my father.

mat

A **mat** is something that covers part

of the floor. We clean our feet on the **mat**.

me

I like my dog. My dog likes **me** too.

mom

Mom is another name for mother.

My **mom** and dad are very nice.

mother

A **mother** is a woman with one
or more children.
My **mother** and father work at home.

my

This coat belongs to me. It is **my** coat.

nice

Nice means kind. Our teacher is **nice**.

no

I wanted to go to the park.
Mom said, "**No**." I did not go to the park.

not

I am short. I am **not** tall.

now

It is snowing as I write this.

It is snowing **now**.

off

1) I turn the light on at night to read.

   I turn the light **off** to sleep.

2) The book dropped from the shelf.

   The book fell **off** the shelf.

on

1) I can't see with the lights off.

   I can see well with the lights **on**.

2) My hat blew off my head.

   I put the hat back **on**.

one

One is a number. It looks like **1**.

You have two eyes but only **one** nose.

our

This game belongs to us. It is **our** game.

out

We don't want to stay in the house.
We will go **out** in the yard to play.

pan

A **pan** is made of metal.
We cook food in a **pan** on top of the stove.

pat

Pat means to touch lightly with your hand.
Let's **pat** the dog.

pet

Any animal that you keep in your home
is a **pet**. We have a turtle as a **pet**.

play

Play means to do something for fun.
Let's **play** with the ball.

pot

A **pot** is a pan with tall sides.
We cook soup in a **pot**.

put

I need a place for my bird cage.
I will **put** it on the table.

ran

Ran means went fast with your legs.
Kim **ran** to school because she was late.

rat

A **rat** is an animal.
A **rat** looks like a big mouse.

red

Red is a color. Stop signs are **red.**

run

Run means to go fast with your legs.

Let's **run** all the way home.

said

The teacher spoke to her class.

She **said**, "Good morning, children."

sand

Sand is made of very tiny stones.

The beach is covered with **sand**.

sat

The teacher told us to sit in our chairs.

We **sat** in them until the lunch bell rang.

saw

I see the moon tonight.

I **saw** the moon last night too.

school

A **school** is a place where we learn things.

Who is your teacher at **school**?

see

See means to look at.

Did you **see** the big fish?

she

Kate is here. **She** came to see us.

sit

I will rest in this chair.

I will **sit** in the chair.

snow

Snow is soft white pieces of ice.

It falls from the sky and covers the ground.

The **snow** was very deep this winter.

so

It is very cold out today.

It is **so** cold today.

sun

The **sun** moves across the sky every day.

It looks like a ball of fire.

The **sun** gives us light and heat.

tell

Tell means to talk about.

Our teacher will **tell** us about her trip.

that

My cup is blue. I like **that** color.

the

I don't want just any pen.

I want **the** green pen.

them

I see Roberto and Rosa across the park.

I see **them**, but they do not see me.

then

1) My dog and I were the same size when
   I was two. I was smaller **then**.

2) I saw the sun go down.
   Then I saw the moon rise.

there

I am at home now. Soon I will go to school.

I will go from here to **there**.

they

Kelly and Tim are playing.
They are having fun!

thing

A **thing** is not a person or animal.

A toy is a **thing**.

this

I am having fun on the ride we are on.

I like **this** ride.

to

Nick lives across the street.

I cross the street when I go **to** his house.

top

Top means the highest part of something.

Can you climb to the **top** of the hill?

toy

A **toy** is something to play with.

A doll is a **toy**.

up

Let's walk from the bottom of the hill

to the top. Let's walk **up** the hill.

147

us

We would like to hear a story.
Please tell **us** a story.

was

I am not sick today. I **was** sick yesterday.

we

You and I are friends. **We** are friends.

went

We go to Grandmother's house every Sunday.
We **went** to her house last Sunday.

when

I don't know what time the party begins.
Do you know **when** the party begins?

will

We are going for a ride after school.
We **will** go for a ride.

with

My mom and I went for a walk together.
I went **with** my mom for a walk.

yes

I asked Mom and Dad if I could go out after dinner. They said, "**Yes**."
I played in the yard until dark.

you

I am fine today. How are **you**?

your

Does this ball belong to you?
Is it **your** ball?

Pretest

Lesson 12

_____

– – – – – – – – – – –

_____

– – – – – – – – – – –

_____

– – – – – – – – – – –

_____

– – – – – – – – – – –

_____

– – – – – – – – – – –

_____

– – – – – – – – – – –

Other Word Forms

_____

– – – – – – – – – – –

_____

_____

_____

– – – – – – – – – – –

Lesson 13

_____

– – – – – – – – – – –

_____

– – – – – – – – – – –

_____

– – – – – – – – – – –

_____

– – – – – – – – – – –

_____

– – – – – – – – – – –

_____

– – – – – – – – – – –

Other Word Forms

_____

– – – – – – – – – – –

_____

_____

_____

– – – – – – – – – – –

Pretest

Lesson 14

_____
— — — — — — — — — —
_____
_____
— — — — — — — — — —
_____
_____
— — — — — — — — — —
_____
_____
— — — — — — — — — —
_____
_____
— — — — — — — — — —
_____

Other Word Forms
_____
— — — — — — — — — —
_____
— — — — — — — — — —
_____
— — — — — — — — — —

Lesson 15

_____
— — — — — — — — — —
_____
_____
— — — — — — — — — —
_____
_____
— — — — — — — — — —
_____
_____
— — — — — — — — — —
_____
_____
— — — — — — — — — —
_____

Other Word Forms
_____
— — — — — — — — — —
_____
— — — — — — — — — —
_____
— — — — — — — — — —

Pretest

Lesson 17

_____

- - - - - - - - - - - - -

_____

- - - - - - - - - - - - -

_____

_____

- - - - - - - - - - - - -

_____

_____

- - - - - - - - - - - - -

_____

_____

- - - - - - - - - - - - -

_____

_____

- - - - - - - - - - - - -

_____

Other Word Forms

_____

- - - - - - - - - - - - -

_____

_____

_____

- - - - - - - - - - - - -

_____

Lesson 18

_____

- - - - - - - - - - - - -

_____

- - - - - - - - - - - - -

_____

_____

- - - - - - - - - - - - -

_____

_____

- - - - - - - - - - - - -

_____

_____

- - - - - - - - - - - - -

_____

_____

- - - - - - - - - - - - -

_____

Other Word Forms

_____

- - - - - - - - - - - - -

_____

_____

_____

- - - - - - - - - - - - -

_____

Pretest

Lesson 19

_____

– – – – – – – – – –

_____

_____

– – – – – – – – – –

_____

_____

– – – – – – – – – –

_____

_____

– – – – – – – – – –

_____

_____

– – – – – – – – – –

_____

Other Word Forms

_____

– – – – – – – – – –

_____

– – – – – – – – – –

_____

– – – – – – – – – –

_____

Lesson 20

_____

– – – – – – – – – –

_____

_____

– – – – – – – – – –

_____

_____

– – – – – – – – – –

_____

_____

– – – – – – – – – –

_____

_____

– – – – – – – – – –

_____

Other Word Forms

_____

– – – – – – – – – –

_____

– – – – – – – – – –

_____

– – – – – – – – – –

_____

Pretest

Lesson 22

_____
— — — — — — — —
_____
— — — — — — — —
_____
— — — — — — — —
_____
— — — — — — — —
_____
— — — — — — — —
_____
— — — — — — — —
_____
— — — — — — — —

Other Word Forms

_____
— — — — — — — —
_____
— — — — — — — —
_____
— — — — — — — —

Lesson 23

_____
— — — — — — — —
_____
— — — — — — — —
_____
— — — — — — — —
_____
— — — — — — — —
_____
— — — — — — — —
_____
— — — — — — — —
_____
— — — — — — — —

Other Word Forms

_____
— — — — — — — —
_____
— — — — — — — —
_____
— — — — — — — —

Pretest

Lesson 24

_____

_ _ _ _ _ _ _ _ _ _ _

_____

_ _ _ _ _ _ _ _ _ _ _

_____

_ _ _ _ _ _ _ _ _ _ _

_____

_ _ _ _ _ _ _ _ _ _ _

_____

_ _ _ _ _ _ _ _ _ _ _

_____

_ _ _ _ _ _ _ _ _ _ _

Other Word Forms

_____

_ _ _ _ _ _ _ _ _ _ _

_____

_ _ _ _ _ _ _ _ _ _ _

_____

_ _ _ _ _ _ _ _ _ _ _

Lesson 25

_____

_ _ _ _ _ _ _ _ _ _ _

_____

_ _ _ _ _ _ _ _ _ _ _

_____

_ _ _ _ _ _ _ _ _ _ _

_____

_ _ _ _ _ _ _ _ _ _ _

_____

_ _ _ _ _ _ _ _ _ _ _

_____

_ _ _ _ _ _ _ _ _ _ _

Other Word Forms

_____

_ _ _ _ _ _ _ _ _ _ _

_____

_ _ _ _ _ _ _ _ _ _ _

_____

_ _ _ _ _ _ _ _ _ _ _

Pretest

Lesson 27

Lesson 28

Other Word Forms

Other Word Forms

Pretest

Lesson 29

_____

- - - - - - - -

_____

- - - - - - - -

_____

- - - - - - - -

_____

_____

- - - - - - - -

_____

_____

- - - - - - - -

_____

Other Word Forms

_____

- - - - - - - -

_____

_____

- - - - - - - -

_____

_____

Lesson 30

_____

- - - - - - - -

_____

_____

_____

- - - - - - - -

_____

_____

- - - - - - - -

_____

_____

- - - - - - - -

_____

Other Word Forms

_____

- - - - - - - -

_____

_____

- - - - - - - -

_____

_____

Pretest

Lesson 32

_____

– – – – – – – – – – – –

_____

– – – – – – – – – – – –

_____

– – – – – – – – – – – –

_____

– – – – – – – – – – – –

_____

– – – – – – – – – – – –

_____

Other Word Forms

_____

– – – – – – – – – – – –

_____

_____

– – – – – – – – – – – –

_____

– – – – – – – – – – – –

_____

Lesson 33

_____

– – – – – – – – – – – –

_____

_____

_____

_____

_____

_____

– – – – – – – – – – – –

_____

_____

– – – – – – – – – – – –

_____

Other Word Forms

_____

– – – – – – – – – – – –

_____

_____

– – – – – – – – – – – –

_____

_____

– – – – – – – – – – – –

_____

Pretest

Lesson 34

_____

Other Word Forms

_____

Lesson 35

_____

Other Word Forms

_____

Posttest

Lesson 12

_____

- - - - - - - - - - - -

_____

- - - - - - - - - - - -

_____

- - - - - - - - - - - -

_____

_____

_____

_____

- - - - - - - - - - - -

_____

- - - - - - - - - - - -

_____

Other Word Forms

_____

- - - - - - - - - - - -

_____

_____

- - - - - - - - - - - -

_____

- - - - - - - - - - - -

_____

Lesson 13

_____

- - - - - - - - - - - -

_____

_____

_____

_____

_____

- - - - - - - - - - - -

_____

_____

- - - - - - - - - - - -

_____

Other Word Forms

_____

- - - - - - - - - - - -

_____

_____

_____

- - - - - - - - - - - -

_____

Posttest

Lesson 14

_____

– – – – – – – – – – – –

_____

– – – – – – – – – – – –

_____

– – – – – – – – – – – –

_____

– – – – – – – – – – – –

_____

– – – – – – – – – – – –

_____

– – – – – – – – – – – –

_____

Other Word Forms

_____

– – – – – – – – – – – –

_____

_____

– – – – – – – – – – – –

_____

– – – – – – – – – – – –

_____

Lesson 15

_____

– – – – – – – – – – – –

_____

– – – – – – – – – – – –

_____

– – – – – – – – – – – –

_____

– – – – – – – – – – – –

_____

– – – – – – – – – – – –

_____

– – – – – – – – – – – –

_____

Other Word Forms

_____

– – – – – – – – – – – –

_____

_____

– – – – – – – – – – – –

_____

– – – – – – – – – – – –

_____

Posttest

Lesson 17

_____

– – – – – – – – – –

_____

– – – – – – – – – –

_____

– – – – – – – – – –

_____

– – – – – – – – – –

_____

– – – – – – – – – –

_____

– – – – – – – – – –

_____

– – – – – – – – – –

Other Word Forms

_____

– – – – – – – – – –

_____

– – – – – – – – – –

_____

– – – – – – – – – –

Lesson 18

_____

– – – – – – – – – –

_____

– – – – – – – – – –

_____

– – – – – – – – – –

_____

– – – – – – – – – –

_____

– – – – – – – – – –

_____

– – – – – – – – – –

_____

– – – – – – – – – –

Other Word Forms

_____

– – – – – – – – – –

_____

– – – – – – – – – –

_____

– – – – – – – – – –

Posttest

Lesson 19

_____

– – – – – – – – – – – – – – – –

_____

– – – – – – – – – – – – – – – –

_____

– – – – – – – – – – – – – – – –

_____

– – – – – – – – – – – – – – – –

_____

– – – – – – – – – – – – – – – –

_____

– – – – – – – – – – – – – – – –

_____

Other Word Forms

_____

– – – – – – – – – – – – – – – –

_____

– – – – – – – – – – – – – – – –

_____

– – – – – – – – – – – – – – – –

_____

Lesson 20

_____

– – – – – – – – – – – – – – – –

_____

– – – – – – – – – – – – – – – –

_____

– – – – – – – – – – – – – – – –

_____

– – – – – – – – – – – – – – – –

_____

– – – – – – – – – – – – – – – –

_____

– – – – – – – – – – – – – – – –

_____

Other Word Forms

_____

– – – – – – – – – – – – – – – –

_____

– – – – – – – – – – – – – – – –

_____

– – – – – – – – – – – – – – – –

_____

Posttest

Lesson 22

_____

- - - - - - - - - - - -

_____

- - - - - - - - - - - -

_____

- - - - - - - - - - - -

_____

- - - - - - - - - - - -

_____

- - - - - - - - - - - -

_____

- - - - - - - - - - - -

_____

Other Word Forms

_____

- - - - - - - - - - - -

_____

_____

_____

- - - - - - - - - - - -

_____

Lesson 23

_____

- - - - - - - - - - - -

_____

- - - - - - - - - - - -

_____

- - - - - - - - - - - -

_____

- - - - - - - - - - - -

_____

- - - - - - - - - - - -

_____

- - - - - - - - - - - -

_____

Other Word Forms

_____

- - - - - - - - - - - -

_____

_____

_____

- - - - - - - - - - - -

_____

Posttest

Lesson 24

_____

- - - - - - - -

_____

- - - - - - - -

_____

- - - - - - - -

_____

- - - - - - - -

_____

- - - - - - - -

_____

- - - - - - - -

_____

Other Word Forms

_____

- - - - - - - -

_____

_____

- - - - - - - -

_____

Lesson 25

_____

- - - - - - - -

_____

- - - - - - - -

_____

- - - - - - - -

_____

- - - - - - - -

_____

- - - - - - - -

_____

- - - - - - - -

_____

Other Word Forms

_____

- - - - - - - -

_____

_____

- - - - - - - -

_____

Posttest

Lesson 27

_____

- - - - - - - - - - - - - - - -

_____

- - - - - - - - - - - - - - - -

_____

- - - - - - - - - - - - - - - -

_____

- - - - - - - - - - - - - - - -

_____

- - - - - - - - - - - - - - - -

_____

- - - - - - - - - - - - - - - -

Other Word Forms

_____

- - - - - - - - - - - - - - - -

_____

_____

_____

- - - - - - - - - - - - - - - -

_____

Lesson 28

_____

- - - - - - - - - - - - - - - -

_____

- - - - - - - - - - - - - - - -

_____

- - - - - - - - - - - - - - - -

_____

- - - - - - - - - - - - - - - -

_____

- - - - - - - - - - - - - - - -

_____

- - - - - - - - - - - - - - - -

Other Word Forms

_____

- - - - - - - - - - - - - - - -

_____

_____

_____

- - - - - - - - - - - - - - - -

_____

Posttest

Lesson 29

_____

- - - - - - - - -

_____

- - - - - - - - -

_____

- - - - - - - - -

_____

- - - - - - - - -

_____

- - - - - - - - -

_____

- - - - - - - - -

_____

Other Word Forms

_____

- - - - - - - - -

_____

- - - - - - - - -

_____

- - - - - - - - -

Lesson 30

_____

- - - - - - - - -

_____

- - - - - - - - -

_____

- - - - - - - - -

_____

- - - - - - - - -

_____

- - - - - - - - -

_____

- - - - - - - - -

_____

Other Word Forms

_____

- - - - - - - - -

_____

- - - - - - - - -

_____

- - - - - - - - -

Posttest

Lesson 32

_____
— — — — — — — — — — — —
_____
— — — — — — — — — — — —
_____
— — — — — — — — — — — —
_____
— — — — — — — — — — — —
_____
— — — — — — — — — — — —
_____
— — — — — — — — — — — —

Other Word Forms
_____
— — — — — — — — — — — —
_____
— — — — — — — — — — — —
_____
— — — — — — — — — — — —

Lesson 33

_____
— — — — — — — — — — — —
_____
— — — — — — — — — — — —
_____
— — — — — — — — — — — —
_____
— — — — — — — — — — — —
_____
— — — — — — — — — — — —
_____
— — — — — — — — — — — —

Other Word Forms
_____
— — — — — — — — — — — —
_____
— — — — — — — — — — — —
_____
— — — — — — — — — — — —

Posttest

Lesson 34

_____

- - - - - - - - - - -

_____

- - - - - - - - - - -

_____

- - - - - - - - - - -

_____

- - - - - - - - - - -

_____

- - - - - - - - - - -

_____

Other Word Forms

_____

- - - - - - - - - - -

_____

_____

- - - - - - - - - - -

_____

- - - - - - - - - - -

_____

Lesson 35

_____

- - - - - - - - - - -

_____

- - - - - - - - - - -

_____

- - - - - - - - - - -

_____

- - - - - - - - - - -

_____

- - - - - - - - - - -

_____

Other Word Forms

_____

- - - - - - - - - - -

_____

_____

- - - - - - - - - - -

_____

- - - - - - - - - - -

_____

Words to Learn Sheet

Name _____

A
_____

- -
_____
- -
_____
_____
- -
_____

B
_____
- -
_____
- -
_____
- -
_____
- -
_____

C
_____
- -
_____
- -
_____
_____
- -
_____

D
- -
_____
- -
_____
- -
_____
- -
_____

Words to Learn Sheet

Name _____

E-F _____

— — — — — — — — — — — — — — —

_____

— — — — — — — — — — — — — — —

_____

— — — — — — — — — — — — — — —

_____

— — — — — — — — — — — — — — —

_____

— — — — — — — — — — — — — — —

G _____

— — — — — — — — — — — — — — —

_____

— — — — — — — — — — — — — — —

_____

— — — — — — — — — — — — — — —

_____

— — — — — — — — — — — — — — —

_____

— — — — — — — — — — — — — — —

H _____

— — — — — — — — — — — — — — —

_____

— — — — — — — — — — — — — — —

_____

— — — — — — — — — — — — — — —

_____

— — — — — — — — — — — — — — —

_____

— — — — — — — — — — — — — — —

_____

— — — — — — — — — — — — — — —

_____

— — — — — — — — — — — — — — —

_____

— — — — — — — — — — — — — — —

_____

— — — — — — — — — — — — — — —

_____

Words to Learn Sheet

Name _____

I-J _____   **M** _____

K-L _____

Words to Learn Sheet

Name _____

N _____

P _____

O _____

Q-R _____

Words to Learn Sheet

Name _____

S _____   **T** _____

_ _ _ _ _ _ _ _ _ _ _ _ _   _ _ _ _ _ _ _ _ _ _ _ _ _

_____   _____

_ _ _ _ _ _ _ _ _ _ _ _ _   _ _ _ _ _ _ _ _ _ _ _ _ _

_____   _____

_ _ _ _ _ _ _ _ _ _ _ _ _   _ _ _ _ _ _ _ _ _ _ _ _ _

_____   _____

_ _ _ _ _ _ _ _ _ _ _ _ _   _ _ _ _ _ _ _ _ _ _ _ _ _

_____   _____

_ _ _ _ _ _ _ _ _ _ _ _ _   _ _ _ _ _ _ _ _ _ _ _ _ _

_____   _____

_ _ _ _ _ _ _ _ _ _ _ _ _   _ _ _ _ _ _ _ _ _ _ _ _ _

_____   _____

_ _ _ _ _ _ _ _ _ _ _ _ _   _ _ _ _ _ _ _ _ _ _ _ _ _

_____   _____

_ _ _ _ _ _ _ _ _ _ _ _ _   _ _ _ _ _ _ _ _ _ _ _ _ _

_____   _____

Words to Learn Sheet

Name _____

U-V

_____

_ _ _ _ _ _ _ _ _ _ _ _ _ _ _ _ _ _

_____

_ _ _ _ _ _ _ _ _ _ _ _ _ _ _ _ _ _

_____

_ _ _ _ _ _ _ _ _ _ _ _ _ _ _ _ _ _

_____

_ _ _ _ _ _ _ _ _ _ _ _ _ _ _ _ _ _

_____

_ _ _ _ _ _ _ _ _ _ _ _ _ _ _ _ _ _

W

_____

_ _ _ _ _ _ _ _ _ _ _ _ _ _ _ _ _ _

_____

_ _ _ _ _ _ _ _ _ _ _ _ _ _ _ _ _ _

_____

_ _ _ _ _ _ _ _ _ _ _ _ _ _ _ _ _ _

_____

_ _ _ _ _ _ _ _ _ _ _ _ _ _ _ _ _ _

_____

X-Y-Z

_____

_ _ _ _ _ _ _ _ _ _ _ _ _ _ _ _ _ _

_____

_ _ _ _ _ _ _ _ _ _ _ _ _ _ _ _ _ _

_____

_ _ _ _ _ _ _ _ _ _ _ _ _ _ _ _ _ _

_____

_ _ _ _ _ _ _ _ _ _ _ _ _ _ _ _ _ _

_____

_ _ _ _ _ _ _ _ _ _ _ _ _ _ _ _ _ _

_____

_____

_ _ _ _ _ _ _ _ _ _ _ _ _ _ _ _ _ _

_____

_ _ _ _ _ _ _ _ _ _ _ _ _ _ _ _ _ _

_____

_ _ _ _ _ _ _ _ _ _ _ _ _ _ _ _ _ _

_____

Lesson	Test	Date	Progress Chart
12	Pretest		
	Posttest		
13	Pretest		
	Posttest		
14	Pretest		
	Posttest		
15	Pretest		
	Posttest		
17	Pretest		
	Posttest		
18	Pretest		
	Posttest		
19	Pretest		
	Posttest		
20	Pretest		
	Posttest		
22	Pretest		
	Posttest		
23	Pretest		
	Posttest		